...stablished
...vel brands,
...s in travel.

...years our
...he secrets
...the world,
...wealth of
...for travel.

**Rely on Thomas Cook as your
travelling companion on your next trip
and benefit from our unique heritage.**

Thomas Cook **pocket** guides

WINDSOR

Your travelling companion since 1873

Written by Robert Savage

Published by Thomas Cook Publishing
A division of Thomas Cook Tour Operations Limited
Company registration no. 3772199 England
The Thomas Cook Business Park, Unit 9, Coningsby Road,
Peterborough PE3 8SB, United Kingdom
Email: books@thomascook.com, Tel: +44 (0) 1733 416477
www.thomascookpublishing.com

Produced by Cambridge Publishing Management Limited
Burr Elm Court, Main Street, Caldecote CB23 7NU
www.cambridgepm.co.uk

ISBN: 978-1-84848-494-8

This first edition © 2011 Thomas Cook Publishing
Text © Thomas Cook Publishing
Cartography supplied by Redmoor Design, Tavistock, Devon
Map data © OpenStreetMap contributors CC-BY-SA, www.openstreetmap.org,
www.creativecommons.org

Series Editor: Karen Beaulah
Production/DTP: Steven Collins

Printed and bound in Spain by GraphyCems

Cover photography © Patrick Ward/Alamy

CONTENTS

SYMBOLS KEY

The following symbols are used throughout this book:

ⓐ address　ⓣ telephone　ⓦ website address　ⓔ email
ⓛ opening times　ⓝ public transport connections　❶ important

The following symbols are used on the maps:

𝒊	information office	▪	point of interest
✚	hospital	=	motorway
🛡	police station	—	main road
🚌	bus station		minor road
🚆	railway station	—	railway
✝	cathedral		

❶ numbers denote featured cafés, restaurants & venues

PRICE CATEGORIES

The ratings below indicate average price rates for a double
room per night, including breakfast:
£ under £99　**££** £100–150　**£££** over £150
The typical cost for a three-course meal without drinks
is as follows:
£ under £20　**££** £20–30　**£££** over £30

▶ *It's not hard to imagine why this is the Queen's favourite weekend home*

INTRODUCING
Windsor

Introduction

You can't say the word Windsor without conjuring up images of the grand **Windsor Castle**, the royal family, horse racing and **Eton College**. The **Changing of the Guard**, the humongous hats designed for **Royal Ascot** and horse-drawn carriages dashing through the cobbled streets are common sights here, and the town thrives on this rich cultural heritage.

Residents of the Royal Borough are proud of their town and with good reason. Windsor is after all one of the most popular tourist destinations in the United Kingdom, and indeed the world. A stroll along the banks of the **River Thames** and a meander through the historic town centre will explain in seconds why so many travellers are drawn here, and just how quintessentially British the town is.

The international landscape might have changed since William the Conqueror established the town, but most of the amazing architecture, the parks and the town's rich cultural inheritance remain.

The shop where H G Wells worked on *The War of the Worlds* and the castle library where Shakespeare wrote *The Merry Wives of Windsor* exemplify Windsor's literary legacy, and you won't go far without recognising a familiar scene from one of the many Hollywood blockbusters that have been filmed in the town.

The River Thames is a big part of local life and hundreds of spectators are drawn down to its banks when the rowing teams from Eton College take to the water, and when the celebrities who own a home on White Lilies Island come to town. Windsor isn't just a holiday home for the Queen, after all.

The permanent residents are a big part of the town's charm too, and you won't be left looking at a map for long before a passer-by stops to offer guidance. Add to this an abundance of quaint one-of-a-kind shops, a local culinary scene headed up by the likes of Heston Blumenthal and the excellent shows taking to the stage at the Theatre Royal, and you have a reasonable idea of the treats that lie in store for you in Windsor.

🔺 *The Changing of the Guard is a world-famous tradition*

When to go

The jam-packed annual events calendar in Windsor means that there's always something going on in the area to suit all tastes and budgets. From the free polo matches on **Smith's Lawn** in **Windsor Great Park** between April and September to the big **Windsor Festival** in September and October, there really is something here for everyone. The weather, like many of the attractions in the Royal Borough, is typically British and can change in a moment, so expect unexpected sunshine and always bring an umbrella. The summer months are particularly popular with outdoor sport enthusiasts, who flock to the area to enjoy the facilities built for the **2012 Olympic Games**.

ANNUAL EVENTS

January–March In January the biggest celebrations in town are the New Year and Chinese New Year parties – the latter sometimes falling in February instead. These are soon followed by the popular Flippin' Windsor and Eton Pancake Challenge. In March look out for the Windsor Festival Spring Weekend, the Italian Market and the opening day of Legoland.

April–June April is all about the Easter events on the High Street and in Windsor Great Park, not to mention the celebrations surrounding the Queen's birthday. May brings with it the Royal Windsor Tattoo and Horse Show, and June kick-starts the summer with Tango on the Bridge, the Royal Windsor Triathlon and Garter Day at the castle. The biggest event of June, however, is Royal Ascot – four days of horse racing attended by the royal family.

July–September In July make time for Cartier International Polo in Windsor Great Park and in August enjoy the Windsor Beer and Jazz Festival in Alexandra Gardens. September brings the Windsor Half Marathon and the first half of the annual Windsor Festival.

October–December After the Windsor Festival wraps up, calendar highlights in October include the Willmott Dixon Day – with a food fair and racing at Ascot. In November the Christmas Shopping Village arrives and the Christmas lights are switched on in Windsor and Eton. In December The Savill Garden leads the festive charge with a packed events programme, the Windsor Reindeer Parade trots through town and the Christmas markets arrive.

● *Windsor High Street plays host to many a celebration*

History

The history of Windsor – which lies less than 34 km (21 miles) away from London – is one of a settlement that has enjoyed many powerful, often royal, connections, including such major figures as William the Conqueror, Henry VIII, Queen Victoria and the current royal family. The town is very much part of Britain's historical fabric.

Windsor has played a crucial role in the evolution of Great Britain – a role that can be traced back to the Battle of Hastings in 1066. William the Conqueror's rapid military success left him with the problem of occupying a foreign land with a hostile population. His forces were spread too thin to accomplish this by numbers alone and so a secure network of fortresses was constructed in order to provide security, and maintain his authority.

Three fortresses, including the Tower of London, were built around the British capital, and in turn were reinforced by another ring of battlements – approximately 32 km (20 miles) or one day's march away. Windsor was the site of one such fortress: occupying an easily defendable chalk outcrop high above the River Thames. The river's proximity was an important part of the decision to choose Windsor as a second line of defence – given its use for transportation and as an essential lifeline to London.

William's Saxon predecessors had constructed their defences nearby in the ancient settlement of Windlesora, now known as Old Windsor. This was later abandoned, but the name was transferred to the newer settlement and shortened over time. Over the years the castle evolved from a wooden fortress to the solid stone

🔺 *The town boasts a long history of royal connections*

building it is today and, in the ten centuries that it has been occupied, the castle has only been laid siege to on two occasions.

The town around the castle also evolved – an accomplishment all the more remarkable given the absence of any manufacturing industry. In fact, to this day, the majority of industry in the area is found in the neighbouring town of Slough. This includes the Mars Bar factory, a facility capable of producing millions upon millions of chocolate bars every year.

Today the town thrives on its cultural legacy and the visitors this attracts – a prosperity threatened only by events such as the devastating fire that almost destroyed Windsor Castle in 1992. The rebuilding work took many years and a staggering £37 million, but the newly restored castle still stands proud over the Royal Borough of Windsor and Maidenhead.

Culture

The most famous facet of Windsor's culture is undeniably the family that takes its name from the town – the Windsors. It is, after all, the royal family that attracts visitors from all over the world to see the artworks, extravagant gifts from foreign heads of state and the coats of armour on display in the living quarters, dressing rooms, galleries and corridors of Windsor Castle. Add to that the spectacular Changing of the Guard, the Queen's penchant for horse racing at Royal Ascot and royal weddings at the Guildhall, and it becomes clear how intrinsic the Windsors are to the culture of the town.

The **Theatre Royal** is also a key component in the culture of Windsor, but the Queen and her family might find it more difficult than usual to see one of the many excellent local productions and West End shows here; ironically, the theatre has no 'royal box'.

The ever-changing multimedia exhibitions and live performances at **The Firestation Centre for Arts and Culture** are a real treat for entertainment seekers, and over the river in Eton the abundant art galleries are filled with contemporary masterpieces. The competition fever that surrounds the boat-racing clubs from Eton College is also a huge part of the town's make-up, and serves as a further cultural enticement.

To top it all off, visitors will be delighted to discover a vibrant culinary culture that thrives on both sides of the Thames and guarantees to satisfy all palates and budgets.

The castle sits in beautiful and extensive grounds

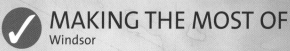

MAKING THE MOST OF
Windsor

Shopping

Shopping might not seem like the most obvious pastime for visitors to Windsor, but with the sheer volume of specialist retailers, travelling markets and one-of-a-kind shops throughout the town, it's hard not to set aside some time for a spot of retail therapy.

Peascod Street is the best place to start for shopaholics visiting Windsor for the first time and it's on this car-free street where you can find the best mix of high-street brands, including Marks & Spencer, and local department stores such as Daniel. There's also a Fenwick department store in the area known as **King Edward Court**. This runs parallel to Peascod Street and is connected to Windsor & Eton Central Rail.

Heading along Peascod Street and away from the castle will take bargain hunters to **Lower Peascod Street** and **St Leonards Road**. Here local craft shops, fine food stores, jewellery makers and florists abound, and at every turn there's a quaint café offering sanctuary from those draining credit-card workouts. The **Windsor Royal Shopping** arcade also has a great range of outlets. As busy as the **high streets** in Eton and Windsor might be, the two shouldn't be overlooked, especially if you're on the hunt for locally produced woollens, pottery and other fine Windsor fare to take away as gifts.

If markets are more to your liking, then the **Ascot Farmers' Market** on the third Sunday of each month at Ascot Racecourse is a must. This is a highlight on the local shopping scene – similar in size and variety to the much-admired **Thames Valley Farmers' Co-operative Market**, which you'll find on St Leonards Road on the first Saturday of the month.

⬣ *The hub of Windsor's shopping scene*

Eating & drinking

If you like to eat well, then you are certain to find a café, restaurant or gastro-pub in Windsor that'll fill a hole and have you coming back for more. From top-quality treats at Michelin-rated restaurants to scrumptious budget eats at The Vansittart Arms (affectionately known as The Fancy Tart among locals), there are stops on Windsor's culinary circuit to suit all tastes.

Just like any other large town in the United Kingdom, you can expect to find your fair share of big-name chain restaurants in key locations across town, but mixed in among these you'll also find a good selection of unique establishments, serving up tasty local produce and extravagant afternoon tea – just as you'd expect in Royal Windsor.

If it's top-notch nosh that you're after, then be sure to phone ahead and try your luck in getting a reservation at The Fat Duck in the nearby village of Bray. The taster menu at Heston Blumenthal's restaurant doesn't come cheap, but it holds three Michelin stars and was voted Best Restaurant in the UK in the 2008 *Good Food Guide*. Or head for The Waterside Inn, also three-Michelin-starred and also in Bray, where the Roux dynasty has presided over exceptional cooking for more than 30 years.

For high-quality dining at a slightly more reasonable price, restaurants such as Strok's Restaurant and The House on the Bridge – both overlooking the River Thames – are a safe bet, and even if you're on a strict budget you can still eat like a king in some great locations. The Two Brewers pub is a prime example of this: located just seconds away from Windsor Great Park, it has a great-value menu.

If you're after a quick bite to eat, the cafés and sandwich shops along St Leonards Road offer a great selection of tasty treats. For something more substantial the arches surrounding Windsor & Eton Central Rail are a good bet, as are the many eateries along Eton High Street.

🔺 The Two Brewers, for good-value British pub grub (see page 67)

Entertainment

The entertainment on offer in Windsor is diverse and plentiful – to the extent that it really would pay dividends to sit down beforehand with a notebook and plan ahead for a day or night out on the town. From the family-friendly **Royal Windsor Wheel** to evening racing at the **Royal Windsor Racecourse**, you'll easily find something to suit all members of the family.

If you are visiting with children, or just want a chance to indulge your own inner child as you stride through exhibitions like a giant, head to **Legoland**, where visitors can learn to drive in fully functional Lego cars before watching the swashbuckling acrobatics of the modern-day Pirates of Skeleton Bay.

If, on the other hand, you prefer a spot of outdoor entertainment and long scenic walks, then **Alexandra Gardens**, **The Brocas**, **The Long Walk** between **Windsor Castle** and **Ascot**, **The Savill Garden** or **The Thames Path** will all serve you well.

If you take your music with a little bit of an edge, the live sets and bands at the **Old Ticket Hall** are super. The same venue also hosts a variety of stand-up comedy acts, that will appeal to many tastes.

If you feel like spending an uplifting evening in the company of some fine thespians, then the **Theatre Royal** is guaranteed to delight – it offers a great mix of West End shows, incredible local talent and international celebrities. Or you can aim to combine it all in one cultural hotspot with a visit to **The Firestation Centre for Arts and Culture**. This is a very contemporary venue where you'll find an amazing blend of films, music, comedy, dance, theatre and art on offer, not to mention good food. If you can't make it to the castle and you only have time for one cultural encounter when you're in town, make sure it's this.

🔺 *Head to the Theatre Royal for a cultural fix*

Sport & relaxation

Hiking & cycling

In addition to exploring Windsor Great Park and The Thames Path on foot, visitors can easily get around on a bicycle. Bikes are available to hire from the Windsor Roller Rink in Alexandra Gardens. And if you prefer to explore using a pair of roller blades or a skateboard, this is also an option. ⓐ Alexandra Gardens ⓣ 01753 830220

Horse riding

Watching the polo matches on Smith's Lawn is a real treat, but so is travelling the length of The Long Walk in Windsor Great Park in your own horse-drawn carriage. It is something of an indulgence and an outing that depends largely on the weather, but if you have your heart set on travelling in style you can arrange this with **Orchard Poyle Horse Carriage Hire** (ⓣ 01784 435983 ⓦ www.orchardpoyle.co.uk). Alternatively, **Ascot Carriages** offer equally exciting excursions and are based at ⓐ The Savill Garden ⓣ 07811 543019 ⓦ www.ascotcarriages.co.uk

Rowing

Eton College Boat Club is based on Dorney Lake, close to Windsor, where the public are always welcome to watch the rowing, canoeing and dragon-boating lessons. The lake also plays host to major sporting events, including the Rowing World Cup. In 2012 it will be a primary venue for the British Olympic and Paralympic Games. ⓐ Eton College Rowing Centre, Dorney ⓣ 01753 832756 ⓦ www.dorneylake.co.uk

Spa treatment

Everyone needs a little indulgence from time to time, and in Windsor one of the most luxurious outlets for such a service is **The Stables Spa** at The Harte and Garter Hotel. As you might gather from the name, the spa is housed in what used to be a stables – 200 years ago, that is. Today the top treatments here include deep-tissue therapy and skin-plumping facials.

🅐 High Street, Windsor 🅣 01753 863426
🅦 www.akkeronhotels.com

🔺 *Anyone for polo?*

Accommodation

Because of Windsor's popularity on the international travel circuit, there are hotels, bed and breakfasts and apartments galore – at prices that will suit everyone. From luxurious hotel suites just over the road from the castle to quiet, chalet-style lodges on Eton High Street and tranquil, secluded offerings just a short distance away, the accommodation pickings are rich – and very often steeped in history, too.

HOTELS

Savill Court Hotel & Spa £–££ A ten-minute journey away from the historic centre of Windsor, the Savill Court Hotel is surrounded by the type of peace and quiet that only 9 ha (22 acres) of privately owned grounds can provide. The spa, with numerous treatment rooms and an indoor pool, is a recent addition to this superb red-brick building, and weekend guests may catch sight of a wedding taking place against the picturesque background. ❸ Bishopsgate, Windsor Great Park ❶ 01784 472000 Ⓦ www.savillcourt.com

The Christopher Hotel ££ This former coaching inn is conveniently located in and among the refined hustle and bustle of Eton High Street. The 34 bedrooms and suites on offer are all decorated to a standard well above the hotel's three-star rating and the beds are comfortable to the point where you'll never want to leave. The superb breakfast and chalet-chic suites are definite strong points at this hotel. ❸ Eton High Street ❶ 01753 852359 Ⓦ www.thechristopher.co.uk

Mercure Windsor Castle Hotel ££ The Mercure Windsor Castle Hotel offers a service that might well receive the royal seal of approval – that is if the Windsors ever grew tired of their castle lodgings. The rooms in this hotel offer a superb view during the Changing of the Guard – and what's on the inside is quite a sight to see, too. The painstakingly preserved Georgian architecture is flawlessly fused with all of the mod cons and, given its proximity to the comings and goings of the High Street, it's refreshingly soundproof too. ⓐ High Street, Windsor ⓣ 01753 851577 ⓦ www.mercure.com

The Oakley Court ££ This rather beautiful French Gothic-style, country house hotel can be found on the outskirts of Windsor, set in 15 ha (37 acres) of landscaped lawns. Guests here will enjoy the excellent selection of rooms, an impressive array of fitness facilities and the AA Rosette Dining Room, not to mention the terrace – a spot perfect for afternoon tea in the great outdoors during the warmer months. ⓐ Windsor Road, Water Oakley ⓣ 01753 609988 ⓦ www.principal-hayley.com

Pinewood Hotel ££ Not far from Windsor and still thoroughly fresh from its renovation in 2005, this four-star hotel offers a tranquil touch of luxury and plenty of space to breathe in its extensive parkland. ⓐ Wexham Park Lane, Slough ⓣ 01753 896400 ⓦ www.pinewoodhotel.co.uk

Royal Adelaide Hotel ££ The Royal Adelaide Hotel is not as close to the castle as some of its counterparts, but it more than makes up for this with the astoundingly good hospitality shown to guests by the staff. A two-minute conversation with the receptionist at this grand hotel will do more for your self-esteem than any self-help book. Recently refurbished bedrooms include flat-screen TVs and Wi-Fi access. ⓐ Kings Road, Windsor ⓣ 01753 863916 ⓦ www.theroyaladelaide.com

Macdonald Windsor Hotel ££–£££ Opened in the summer of 2010, this addition to the accommodation listings in the Royal Borough has been well received – thanks to the 120 luxurious bedrooms and suites, not to mention a key location just opposite the historic Guildhall. If you like boutique hotels that pack a modern punch, then you'll love the Macdonald Windsor Hotel, and the simple but amazing Caleys Lounge and Restaurant on the ground floor. ⓐ High Street, Windsor ⓣ 0844 879 9101 ⓦ www.macdonaldhotels.co.uk

Sir Christopher Wren's House Hotel ££–£££ This elegant town house began life as the home of the famous architect, Sir Christopher Wren (see page 51). Today it's a Grade II-listed building and a hotel that most certainly pushes the boat out. Unique features here include fine dining at the multi-award-winning Strok's Restaurant, and a massage at the Wren's Spa will ensure you feel well and truly relaxed. This is most certainly a high-end option but, nonetheless, a treat worth spending that little bit extra on. ⓐ Thames Street, Windsor ⓣ 01753 861354 ⓦ www.sirchristopherwren.co.uk

The Harte & Garter Hotel and Spa £££ There aren't many hotels where you can wake up from a good night's sleep and open the curtains to spectacular views of Windsor Castle, but that's exactly what you can expect at The Harte & Garter. After a thorough refurbishment in 2007, this four-star lodging offers guests a generous serving of the luxurious and a top location with direct access to the best attractions in town. ⓐ High Street, Windsor ⓣ 01753 863426 ⓦ www.akkeronhotels.com

BED & BREAKFAST

Park Farm £ If you prefer a cosy and informal B&B to a concierge-controlled hotel, you'll enjoy a stay at Park Farm. This family-run business is just off the main shopping strip in Windsor and offers en-suite facilities in every room, along with the option of self-catering accommodation. ⓐ St Leonards Road, Windsor ⓣ 01753 866823 ⓦ www.parkfarm.com

The Rutlands B&B £ The Rutlands B&B is very much all about the Victorian charm that can be found in every facet of this homely building. Whether it's the perfectly polished brass bed knobs or the painted period fireplaces, this terraced building with a balcony will bring a smile to your face. ⓐ St Leonards Road, Windsor ⓣ 01753 859533 ⓦ www.therutlandsbandb.co.uk

SELF-CATERING

Dorney Self-Catering Apartments £ These apartments are located in the beautiful village of Dorney, a few minutes away from Windsor. Guests who stay here will find themselves in the grounds of a picturesque Tudor house, surrounded by luscious and unspoilt English countryside. ⓐ The Old Place, Dorney ⓣ 01753 827037 ⓦ www.troppo.uk.com

THE BEST OF WINDSOR

Windsor is a city where you'll never be bored or stuck for something to do. In fact, there's so much going on that, in order to make the most of your trip, it really does pay to shortlist the cream of the crop.

TOP 10 ATTRACTIONS

- **Theatre Royal** Take in a show at this spectacular setting where, ironically, there's no royal box (see page 67).

- **Windsor Castle** A true beacon of British history, where visitors can explore the State Apartments, Queen Mary's giant Dolls' House and much more (see page 58).

- **Eton College** Established by Henry VI in 1440, Eton is one of the most prestigious, and expensive, schools in the world (see page 73).

- **Windsor Great Park** Over 405 ha (1,000 acres) of beautiful gardens, lakes and woodland span the distance between Windsor Castle and Ascot (see page 53).

- **Legoland** A real treat for all the family: a whole world created from the tiny plastic bricks that everyone loves (see page 56).

- **The Savill Garden** One of the finest ornamental gardens in the UK, home to an extraordinary mix of native and exotic species (see page 57).

- **Peascod Street** A true delight for shopaholics – this pedestrianised strip includes boutique treats and department store fare (see page 61).

- **Royal Ascot** An annual event where the presence of top hats, designer dresses and the royal family is just as important as the horse racing (see page 55).

- **The Thames Path** Britain's greatest river runs through the heart of Windsor, and by it you'll find many miles of beautiful walks and nature trails (see page 53).

- **Eton High Street** Unforgettable architecture, restaurants, one-of-a-kind pubs and more shops than you can shake a stick at (see page 69).

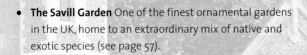

🔻 *Illustrious Eton College*

Suggested itineraries

Tried, tested and tailor-made itineraries, showcasing what you can squeeze into your stay in Windsor.

HALF-DAY: WINDSOR IN A HURRY

If you can only spare a morning or an afternoon for sightseeing in Windsor, then use your time wisely by taking a tour of Windsor Castle and Windsor Great Park. The castle ticks every box with its grand fortress, royal walkways and impressive array of galleries. A stroll through the massive Windsor Great Park is the perfect way to round off any trip and the views of the castle's stone buttresses from The Long Walk – between Windsor Castle and Ascot – are truly superb.

1 DAY: TIME TO SEE A LITTLE MORE

After exploring the castle and the park, take the gate exit on Park Street, walk towards the town centre and stop en route for a drink at the traditional pub The Two Brewers or The Crooked House of Windsor. The latter, a quaint café, was constructed using damp timber; when it dried, it dried crooked. Explore the shops and restaurants in the Windsor Royal Shopping arcade, before returning to the High Street and proceeding down the hill and towards the river. Look out for Sir Christopher Wren's House before you cross the bridge over the water to Eton High Street. In Eton enjoy the art galleries, traditional shops and the beautiful buildings of Eton College, before grabbing a spot of supper from one of the many excellent restaurants nearby. Finish off your day with a show at the Theatre Royal.

2–3 DAYS: SHORT BREAK

In addition to the aforementioned activities, take a stroll along the beautiful Thames Path and linger at Eton College for a guided tour. A visit to Legoland and a horse-drawn carriage ride through Windsor Great Park both also come highly recommended.

LONGER: ENJOYING WINDSOR TO THE FULL

With a bit more time at your disposal, take a jaunt along the river to Maidenhead. For memorable day trips, Hampton Court Palace, the magnificent Cliveden Estate and the Royal Botanic Gardens at Kew are all within easy reach.

⬤ *Traditions die hard on Eton High Street (see page 71)*

Something for nothing

With a bit of local know-how it's easy to experience the best of Windsor – without spending a penny. **The Windsor Heritage Walking Trail** offers visitors a rich mix of sights, cultural inheritance and unique local experiences. From stunning views of the River Thames to historic secrets hidden in the cobbled streets of Guildhall Island, and from the Crooked House to the Curfew Tower – the turret that once housed Windsor Castle's dungeons and from which criminals used to be hanged – this self-guided walk is a real treat. A free guide detailing everything you need to know about the attractions you'll see along the way is available from the **Royal Windsor Information Centre** (🅐 Windsor Royal Shopping ☎ 01753 743900), which is also where the trail begins.

If you enjoy fresh air and walking you are spoilt for choice in this area, with acres of fabulous parkland right on Windsor's doorstep, as well as the picturesque charms of **The Thames Path National Trail** (see page 53). Windsor Great Park and Richmond Park offer space aplenty for roaming and celebrity spotting, as well as stunning views of central London.

There are also plenty of riverside walks that can be enjoyed for free: start in Maidenhead and follow The Thames Path past the magnificent **Cliveden Estate** (see page 80) and on to Cookham and Marlow, attractive and lively towns in their own right. Just south of Maidenhead you can have fun trying out the spectacular **Sounding Arch** (see page 80), built by Isambard Kingdom Brunel – shout up into the bricks and listen to count how many times you can hear your voice echo.

Window shopping can be enjoyed for free, as can a smile at the hefty price tags on the artworks displayed in the galleries lining Eton High Street. The beautiful architecture and interesting shops are attractions in themselves and act as reminders of a more genteel age.

On the Eton side of Windsor Bridge, check out the millennium sculptures designed by Wendy Ramshaw OBE, which make an excellent viewing point across both sides of the river.

◆ *The intriguing sculptures built to celebrate the second millennium*

When it rains

When the great British weather strikes without warning and the heavens open – as they often do – there are plenty of options available for visitors to Windsor. The more prominent attractions include the indoor delights of Windsor Castle (see page 58), not to mention the sheltered itineraries offered by the **French Brothers' boat tours** and the **City Sightseeing bus tours** (see page 46).

Alternatively, you can enjoy a spot of indoor sport at **Windsor Leisure Centre**, where everyone is welcome to come along and participate in the daily classes and fitness events. If you're already soaked to the bone, then you might as well take it one step further and take advantage of the two pools; they appeal to both serious fitness swimmers and to families searching out a bit of fun with a wave machine.

Many visitors also follow the local example when wet weather strikes, by seeking shelter in the many homely cafés that are on offer in the centre of Windsor. St Leonards Road is a great place to go to really soak up the café culture, and offers an international atmosphere in addition to the traditional English tea rooms. Nearby, on Peascod Street, the Daniel department store is a popular indoor retail option.

If your solution to rainy days is to see a good movie, then The Firestation Centre for Arts and Culture (see page 55) offers a good selection of multimedia treats. But if you prefer to catch up with the most recent Hollywood blockbusters, the **Odeon** cinema in the neighbouring town of Maidenhead – a short bus or taxi journey away – is a safe bet.

On arrival

Windsor couldn't be easier to find your way around, and no matter what method of transportation you use to get there – be it train, coach, car or horse-drawn carriage – you'll soon discover that the best way to see the town is on foot. Windsor is perfect for pedestrians – the combination of cobbled streets, pedestrian-only shopping zones, parks and river walks keeps cars at bay and makes any trip here all the more pleasant. This scenic town is also a key spot for avid walkers arriving from the northwest or the southeast via The Thames Path, or embarking on a day's hike from here – but not before devouring a hearty meal at one of the many excellent riverside cafés and restaurants.

Despite the fact that Windsor is definitely geared to those on foot, there are still plenty of parking spaces available for visitors who choose to drive there. Motorists can leave their cars safely while they enjoy the stress-free streets. Furthermore, the many coaches that convey visitors between the town, central London and further afield, nip in and out of the town centre with ease.

It is very difficult to get lost in Windsor with the easy-to-spot, grand castle looming over so much of the town, but if you do become disorientated, or lose sight of the stone turrets as you head towards the bottom end of Peascod Street, don't hesitate to ask for help. The residents of Windsor are courteous through and through, so expect excellent manners, a polite perspective and plenty of assistance.

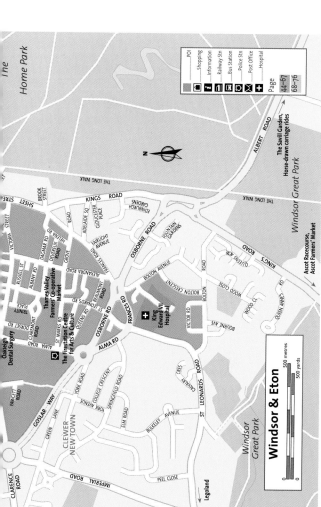

Windsor & Eton

Home Park

Ine

POI
Shopping .... Information
🚉 Railway Stn
🚌 Bus Station
👮 Police Stn
✕ Post Office
✚ Hospital

Page
44–67
68–76

N

ALBERT ROAD

The Savill Garden,
Horse-drawn carriage rides

Windsor Great Park

Ascot Racecourse,
Ascot Farmers' Market

THE LONG WALK

KINGS ROAD

BROOK STREET

SHEET STREET

VICTORIA STREET

EDINBURGH GARDENS

ADELAIDE SQ

GLOUCESTER PLACE

FAIRLIGHT AVENUE

OSBORNE ROAD

FOUNTAIN GARDENS

THE LONG WALK

DACMAR RD

HELENA RD

DEVEREUX ROAD

GROVE

FRANCES ROAD

ALEXANDRA ROAD

RUSSELL ST

ALBANY RD

BOLTON AVENUE

QUEEN'S ACRE

KING'S ROAD

BOLTON CRESCENT

WOOD CLOSE

BOLTON ROAD

Thames Valley
Farmers' Co-operative
Market

TRINITY PLACE

CLAREMONT ROAD

ST MARKS RD

BEAUMONT ROAD

ST LEONARD'S RD

QUEEN'S RD

FRANCES RD

D GROOM

The Firestation Centre
for Arts & Culture

Oakleigh
Dental Surgery

DORSET RD

ALMA ROAD

OSBORNE RD

ALMA RD

✚ King
Edward VII
Hospital

VICTOR RD

BOURNE AVE

QUEEN ANNE'S

FAWCETT ROAD

GOSLAR WAY

YORK ROAD

COLLEGE CRESCENT

SPRINGFIELD ROAD

ELM ROAD

CAVALRY CRES

ST LEONARDS ROAD

GREEN LANE

YORK AVENUE

BULKELEY AVENUE

Windsor
Great Park

CLEWER
NEW TOWN

CLARENCE ROAD

IMPERIAL ROAD

PEEL CLOSE

Legoland

Windsor
Great Park

500 metres
500 yards
0
0

35

ARRIVING

By air

The airport closest to Windsor just happens to be Heathrow, the busiest airport in the world. This has connections to pretty much everywhere that you might need or want to go to. Heathrow Airport is a mere fifteen-minute journey from the centre of the town. Both Gatwick and Luton Airports can also be reached within an hour from Windsor by road.

The most efficient way to travel directly from Heathrow Airport to Windsor is by coach. Express coach services operating on Route 77 provide a direct link between Windsor town centre and Terminal 5 at Heathrow Airport. Coaches between the two locations run every half an hour during the day and once every hour on Sundays and in the evenings. The service drops off and picks up passengers just opposite the parish church on Windsor High Street.

The coach company behind this service is called **First**. You can get more information about the airport transfer service, including timetables, by calling (☎ 0871 200 2233) or by checking online (ⓦ www.firstgroup.com).

Alternatively, **National Express** coach services (ⓦ www. nationalexpress.com) also offer direct airport transfers between Heathrow Airport and Windsor.

By rail

When you take a train to Windsor you will arrive at Windsor & Eton Central Rail or Windsor & Eton Riverside Rail. Both stations are centrally located and are just a few minutes away from the High Street and Windsor Castle.

Windsor & Eton Central Rail – a part of the Windsor Royal Shopping arcade – is the terminus point for a branch line that connects Windsor to the neighbouring borough of Slough. Passengers can change at Slough for frequent services to London Paddington and regular connections to Oxford and Reading. An average journey between London Paddington and Windsor & Eton Central Rail takes around 40 minutes.

Windsor & Eton Riverside Rail is, as the name suggests, located by the river. This is the terminus point for direct services between Windsor and London Waterloo. This route stops at several key locations between Windsor and London, including Richmond and Clapham Junction, the latter a station with a direct link to London's Gatwick Airport. The average journey time between the two ends of this line is one hour.

It should be noted that, even though the two stations are not notorious locations for pickpockets, they can become very crowded, thereby presenting thieves with the opportunity to take advantage of new arrivals. So it does pay to stay safe, and keep an eye on your valuables at all times.

By coach & bus

Travelling by coach is one of the most efficient ways of getting into and out of Windsor. The **Green Line** coach service is one example – it operates a popular and highly reliable service between London Victoria Coach Station and Windsor. Stops along the route of the 701 and 702 Green Line coach services include Hyde Park Corner, Knightsbridge, Kensington and Hammersmith. After Windsor the coaches travel on to Legoland and Bracknell.

National Express coaches connect Windsor to the majority of UK cities and – like most coach services arriving in Windsor – drop off and pick up passengers just opposite the Parish Church on the High Street. There's also a dedicated coach park, used by a number of tour companies, next to Alexandra Gardens.

Local buses are also a very efficient part of Windsor's infrastructure; with an **Explorer FirstDay** ticket, travellers can take advantage of unlimited travel on First coaches and buses within the Royal Borough of Windsor and Maidenhead. The

⬤ *Navigate Windsor atop the City Sightseeing bus*

same ticket can also be used on the local bus network to get as far as Heathrow, Staines, Slough, Bracknell and High Wycombe. Bus tickets, free route maps and more information are available from the Royal Windsor Information Centre.

By car

There's no denying that Windsor is the domain of the pedestrian, but visitors with cars are still well catered for.

Drivers arriving from the M4 motorway should take the junction 6 exit – signposted for Windsor. From the M25 the Windsor exit is junction 13, signposted Egham; on the M3 the exit for Windsor is junction 3, signposted Bagshot. Drivers approaching via the M40 should exit at junction 4, signposted Marlow, or junction 2, signposted Beaconsfield.

When you arrive in Windsor there are three primary car parks – promoted by local authorities – that cater for those who wish to stay in the town for more than two hours. These long-stay facilities work out cheaper than other local alternatives and all three are no more than a ten-minute walk away from Windsor Castle. These parking facilities are signposted on the approach to Windsor as Romney Lock, King Edward VII and Alexandra Gardens.

FINDING YOUR FEET

Windsor and Eton aren't difficult to navigate but, during your first trip to the towns, you never know when a map might be useful. This can be especially true when walking along the Peascod Street shopping strip, where eventually you'll lose sight of the castle, the principal guide to orientation.

New visitors should note that although crime levels in Windsor are relatively low, it's always best to take good care of your personal belongings in crowded places.

ORIENTATION

To get your bearings in Windsor, remember that when you're facing the High Street with the castle behind you, the river and Eton are to your right at the bottom of the hill, the shopping along Peascod Street is linked to the High Street from a road in front of you, and Windsor Great Park is to your left – as you follow the High Street to the point where it joins Park Street.

GETTING AROUND

Windsor and Eton are very easy to get around on foot; however, for journeys a little further afield the local bus services and taxi companies are excellent. The seasonal **City Sightseeing** bus tours also cover the majority of Windsor and Eton, with a hop-on, hop-off service that stops at a number of key locations.

You can catch a cab from the taxi rank on the High Street, just outside Windsor Castle. For advance bookings **Five Star Radio Cars** (☎ 01753 858888) and **Windsor Radio Cars** (☎ 01753 677677) are both recommended.

If you want to hire a car your best bet in the area is **Practical Car & Van Rental** (☎ Vansittart Industrial Estate ☎ 01753 833442 ☎ windsor@practical.co.uk).

▶ *The great bridge connecting Windsor to Eton*

THE CITY OF
Windsor

Introduction to city areas

The town of Windsor is 34 km (21 miles) west of Charing Cross train station in London and is bordered to the north by the River Thames. The river separates Windsor from the town of Eton, a short walk away over the Windsor Bridge. Eton and Windsor are key components in the Royal Borough of Windsor and Maidenhead, and experiencing the two areas together will give any traveller a much greater understanding of this historic part of Great Britain.

The first section covers **Windsor**. Seen from above, Windsor is contained in the east and in the north by the curve of the River Thames. Windsor Great Park occupies much of the town's eastern territory; to the south is Legoland and to the west is the village of Oakley Green. It's within these boundaries that visitors can experience Windsor's rich collection of historical landmarks, the influence of the royal family throughout the ages, extensive walking trails, beautiful parks and a melting pot of contemporary culture.

The second section turns its attention to **Eton**, which stands mere metres north of Windsor over the River Thames. This is a town known throughout the world for its ancient school, Eton College, and the many famous students who have graduated from this institution before going on to accomplish great things in politics, literature, engineering and countless other fields. The town of Eton follows the High Street, which stretches from the Windsor Bridge to the collection of college buildings and school grounds.

⬥ *A decidedly charming and rare Edwardian postbox*

Windsor

It is true that Windsor's biggest attraction is the castle and the historic gems contained within it, but there's also a great deal more to experience and enjoy among the cobbled streets, lovingly tended parks and riverside trails. There are beautiful monuments and stunning structures around every corner and, because of the town's historic importance, every building, walkway, street and sight is preserved, restored and safeguarded for future generations. The town is also home to some of the best international fashion designers, an instantly recognisable café culture and a theatre graced by some of the biggest names in the entertainment business.

SIGHTS & ATTRACTIONS

Alexandra Gardens

In August 1902 the land here was regenerated and trees were planted – an event tied into the celebrations surrounding the coronation of King Edward VII and his queen, Alexandra. A bandstand was also erected to provide a stage for the band of the Royal Horse Guards. Today, visitors can enjoy this protected green space, which includes a special sundial that anyone can use to tell the time by standing on the current month of the year and observing their shadow. Alexandra Gardens is also home to the Royal Windsor Wheel during the summer months and at Christmas. This Ferris wheel is similar in concept, if not in scale, to the London Eye. ⓐ Barry Avenue

The Changing of the Guard

This is a show of pomp and military precision that's unrivalled the world over. The procession of guards along the High Street and into Windsor Castle, where they replace those on duty, is accompanied by a band and culminates at the Guardroom in the castle's Lower Ward. Depending on the weather, the event can be enjoyed at 10.50 from the High Street, with the part of the ceremony that occurs inside the castle starting at 11.00. The old guards march back to their barracks at about 11.25. The parade takes place year-round, but never on a Sunday.

🅐 High Street 🕐 10.50, 11.25 alternate days (Aug–Mar); Mon–Sat (Apr–July) ❶ Admission charge for the part that takes place in Windsor Castle

🔺 Like clockwork, at 11.00

TOURS

City Sightseeing bus tours

You can walk across Windsor town centre in less than 30 minutes, but a number of sights on the outskirts are not so easy to reach. The hop-on, hop-off bus tour takes passengers from Windsor Castle past the Guildhall, Windsor Great Park and the village of Datchet. The route passes through Eton and returns to the town centre via Thames Street. ⓐ High Street, Windsor ⓣ 01708 866000 ⓦ www.city-sightseeing.com ⓛ daily (Mar–Nov); for Dec–Feb listings, check online ⓘ Admission charge

French Brothers' boat tours

French Brothers offer a number of trips, but their 40-minute jaunt is a nice, bite-size treat. A major highlight is the sight of some of the small boats that bear the Cross of St George and the Crest of Dunkirk. These boats took part in Operation Dynamo – a last-minute mission that saved thousands of lives in World War II – when a flotilla of unarmed vessels ferried troops back from the failed 1940 landings in Dunkirk. Other tour highlights include Brunel's famous echoing railway bridge and a number of celebrity homes on White Lilies Island. This spot has been a home to Michael Caine and Natalie Imbruglia. ⓐ Clewer Boathouse, Clewer Court Road ⓣ 01753 851900 ⓦ www.boat-trips.co.uk ⓛ 10.00–17.00 (Apr–Oct); schedule subject to river conditions Nov–Mar ⓘ Admission charge

Horse-drawn carriage rides

The world-famous pictures of Queen Elizabeth riding through Windsor Great Park with President Ronald Reagan portray just how intrinsic horse riding is to the culture of Windsor. A carriage ride through the park is a highlight of any trip and **Ascot Carriages** stands out as a family-run business with a personal touch. Starting from the Savill Building, the ride takes in the beautiful water lilies on the Cow Pond, as well as Chapel Wood – populated by maple trees that turn a fiery red in autumn and an oak tree that's over 400 years old. The carriage used on the tour was passed on from Lt-Col Sir John Miller who was Her Majesty the Queen's Equerry and Horsemaster. ⓐ Wick Lane Englefield Green ⓣ 07811 543019 ⓦ www.ascotcarriages. co.uk ⓛ 11.00–16.00 daily; appointments by arrangement, weather permitting ⓘ Admission charge

Windsor Town Walks

The Windsor Town Walk guides are fonts of knowledge about every nook and cranny in Windsor and often extend the hour-long excursions at no extra cost – simply because they enjoy sharing what they know. They have a store of facts about everything from the madness of King George to the leading role of the royal family in British farming. ⓐ Royal Windsor Information Centre ⓣ 01753 743900 ⓦ www.windsor.gov.uk ⓛ 11.30 Sat & Sun (Apr–Aug), call ahead for availability ⓘ Admission charge

Church Street Gardens

Also known as the Heritage Gardens, this is the smallest public open space in Windsor. A cluster of cottages once occupied this site but, after a fire in 1800, all that remains are the fireplaces on the nearby wall. The gardens offer locals and visitors a cherished sanctuary away from the hustle and bustle of town. A stone hopscotch game displays the shields of the monarchs connected to Windsor. ⓐ Church Street, just off High Street

Glorious Britain shop

It's a little known fact that H G Wells was a resident of Windsor in the late 19th century. While here he worked as a draper's apprentice for Rodgers and Denyer, a company that once occupied what is now the Glorious Britain shop. At the same time Wells was also working on his influential science-fiction masterpiece, *The War of the Worlds*. ⓐ 26 High Street

The Goswells

This patch of land was once a slum. During Queen Victoria's reign it was cleared and developed as a grand and green open space with views of the castle and the river. Today it belongs to the National Trust and visitors can enjoy the bowling green – it is home to Windsor and Eton Bowling Club – and the free tennis courts. You'll also find the **Royal Windsor Maze** in here. ⓐ Goswell Road

Guildhall

This amazing building, designed by Sir Christopher Wren in the 17th century, is perhaps one of the most famous wedding venues in the world. It was in the Ascot Room here that Prince Charles married Camilla Parker Bowles, and where Sir Elton John tied the knot with David Furnish. The interior includes chandeliers on loan from Her Majesty the Queen and, outside, keen observers will spot four rather strange columns. When the building neared completion the local authorities refused to pay Sir Christopher Wren unless he added extra pillars to support the overhang. Despite Sir Christopher's argument that his designs held up thousands of tonnes of masonry in St Paul's Cathedral, his protests fell on deaf ears. He eventually gave in and added the columns – but if you look closely you'll see that they're separated from the ceiling by a very slight gap. The supports are purely aesthetic but the authorities were none the wiser and Sir Christopher got his fee. ⓐ High Street

Guildhall Island

After the Guildhall became a prominent feature of the town in the 17th century, the cobbled streets around it, including Church Street, became known as Guildhall Island. In days gone by this was the town's main market area; in fact, until the 18th century, Church Street was known simply as Fyssh Street because of the quantity (and smell) of the fish that were sold here. The street also has royal connections: on the wall of The Old King's Head you'll find a copy of the death warrant issued for King Charles I (1600–1649), signed by Oliver Cromwell.

Park Street

This street in Windsor looks like any other collection of homes and businesses before you take account of who their next door

Old-fashioned pubs deck the cobbled streets of Guildhall Island

neighbour is. The fact that the British monarch resides only metres away means house prices here are astoundingly high.

The Royals' Royal Mail postboxes

At the High Street's junction with Park Street you'll notice two postboxes, one red and one blue. The blue box is one of the first airmail postboxes in the country. Neither is still in use, but they remain by royal decree. The same protection is behind the survival of the cobbled streets that crisscross Guildhall Island. The cobbles were replaced with a smooth surface decades ago; however, when faced with this affront to their national heritage, the British public turned to the Queen for support. Three weeks later the cobbles were back. The same thing happened when the red telephone boxes began to disappear. ⓐ Park Street

St George's School

This school at the bottom of the Windsor Castle hill was created to provide choirboys for St George's Chapel within the castle. It has supplied the chapel with an uninterrupted line of choristers since 1352 and connects directly to the castle by the House of 100 Steps. ⓐ Windsor Castle

Sir Christopher Wren's House

Sir Christopher Wren was a hugely successful architect in the 17th and 18th centuries and, as you'd expect, the house he built for himself mirrors many of his greatest professional achievements. Not much is known of the history of the Wren family in Windsor beyond projects such as the Guildhall and the role played in the community by Sir Christopher's father, the

Dean of Windsor. Today this Grade II-listed, red-brick building is a hotel (see page 24). ⓐ Thames Street

Statue of Queen Victoria

This grand bronze statue is an unmissable sight on the approach to Windsor and a great photo opportunity for anyone who wants to capture the royal spirit of the town, set against the grand backdrop of Windsor Castle. The statue was commissioned and erected to celebrate Queen Victoria's Golden Jubilee. It was designed by Sir Joseph Edgar Boehm and unveiled to the public in 1887, on the site formerly occupied by the town's market. ⓐ High Street

◆ The towering statue of Queen Victoria

Taxi rank stoppers

Look down at the road by the taxi rank on the High Street and you'll notice a series of metal bars driven into the tarmac. In the days before handbrakes it was somewhat harder to keep a taxi stationary on this incline – especially taxis attached to horses. The bars were therefore installed to prevent the carriages from rolling backwards. ⓐ High Street

The Thames Path National Trail

This popular walking trail follows the 296-km (184-mile) route of the River Thames – from its source in the Cotswolds to London. If you're determined, you can reach central London on foot within a day. If, however, you prefer to keep it local, a popular route stretches between Romney Lock, 4.8 km (3 miles) upriver from the Old Windsor Lock, and Bell Weir Lock, a similar distance downriver. ⓦ www.visitthames.co.uk

The Windsor Bridge Elm Tree

When Dutch elm disease destroyed over 25 million of the UK's elms the future of the tree seemed hopeless, until Prince Charles appealed to the USA and began importing a disease-resistant species from North Carolina. One of the first saplings was planted here in Windsor. ⓐ Windsor Bridge

Windsor Castle & Windsor Great Park

Windsor Castle is undeniably a huge cultural component of the town, but it's also a major sight in its own right (see also Culture, page 58). The Round Tower at the centre dominates any snapshot and has been built up over the years in order to remain the highest point in Windsor. The castle is often likened to a town – given that it occupies 5.25 ha (13 acres) of land and contains a huge array of fascinating facets. The magnificent **State Apartments** and **St George's Chapel** have to be seen to be believed, and just outside of the castle walls **Windsor Great Park** is home to another battery of visual delights. A quick stroll along **The Long Walk** offers spectacular views towards to the castle, the statue of George III on **Snow Hill** and Ascot beyond. Also in the park, it's worth keeping an eye out for the spectacular polo matches on **Smith's Lawn** – between **The Savill Garden** and **The Valley Gardens**. ⓐ High Street

⬥ *Superb views over the grounds and parks that surround the castle*

Windsor Parish Church of St John the Baptist

There's been a church on this spot for over 800 years and visitors can see Saxon arches and Norman architecture preserved in the underground vaults. The original church can be traced back to Henry I (1068–1135), when he moved the royal court from Old Windsor to the castle. Inside the building today, visitors will find a set of ornate glass doors – the Royal Borough's tribute to those who fell in World War II – and a rather famous painting: *The Last Supper* by Benjamin West, presented to the Royal Chapel in 1660 by Brian Duppa, Bishop of Winchester. ⓐ High Street

CULTURE

Ascot Racecourse

This is undoubtedly one of the most famous horse-racing venues in the world. Competitions are held here throughout the year, in addition to a healthy schedule of beer and wine festivals, family days and – of course – Royal Ascot. This event in June is attended by the Queen and many other members of the royal family, and it's during this time that spectators in Windsor Great Park can see the Queen and her horse-drawn entourage leave Windsor Castle and proceed to the racecourse. ⓐ Ascot ⓘ 0870 227 227 ⓦ www.ascot.co.uk ❶ Admission charge

The Firestation Centre for Arts and Culture

There's been an arts centre in this old fire station for almost 40 consecutive years, and the current incarnation is home to an exciting array of films, music, comedy, dance, theatre and art.

Other attractions include monthly book-swap clubs and open-mic nights. ❸ St Leonards Road ❶ 01753 866865 ❿ www.fire stationartscentre.com ❻ 10.00–24.00 Mon–Sat, 11.00–23.00 Sun ❶ Admission charge

Legoland

This land of approximately 55 million Lego bricks is an attraction that brings out the inner child in everyone. Expect interactive exhibits, pirate acrobats and the world's most famous landmarks recreated in miniature. Legoland is worth a

🔺 *A veritable hotbed of all things entertaining*

trip if only to see the diminutive London skyline. ⓐ Winkfield Road
ⓘ 0871 222 2001 ⓦ www.legoland.co.uk ⓗ hours vary daily (Apr–
Nov); closed mid-Nov–Mar ⓝ Bus: shuttle buses operate from both
Windsor & Eton Central Rail and Windsor & Eton Riverside Rail;
Coach: Green Line 701 and 702 ⓘ Admission charge

Royal Windsor Racecourse

What sets Royal Windsor Racecourse apart from its well-known
counterpart in Ascot is the stunning riverside location and the
figure-of-eight layout – and that it stands on one of the largest
islands in the River Thames. There's even a yacht basin for those
arriving by boat. The course was featured in the 2001 film *Last
Orders* starring Bob Hoskins. It offers a year-round racing
schedule. ⓐ Maidenhead Road ⓘ 01753 498400 ⓦ www.
windsor-racecourse.co.uk ⓘ Admission charge

Royal Windsor Wheel

Standing 4 m (13 ft) taller than Nelson's Column, this popular
seasonal attraction is lit up at night by 60,000 LED lights.
The wheel offers great views of Windsor, Eton, the Berkshire
countryside, and even the sparkling skyline of London.
ⓐ Alexandra Gardens ⓘ 020 8241 9818 ⓦ www.royal
windsorwheel.com ⓗ 10.00–22.00 daily (May–Aug); closed
Sept–Apr (excluding Christmas) ⓘ Admission charge

The Savill Garden

A short taxi ride or an enthusiastic hike away from Windsor is
The Savill Garden, a collection that showcases some of the
United Kingdom's most impressive woodland and ornamental

garden species. Rare plants thrive in this 14-ha (35-acre) enclosure and visitors can expect everything from the golden grasslands of New Zealand to giant pumpkins. The 2010 Rose Garden is a beautiful addition to this scenic getaway. ⓐ Wick Lane, Englefield Green ⓣ 01784 435544 ⓦ www.theroyal landscape.co.uk ⓛ 10.00–18.00 daily (Mar–Oct); 10.00–16.30 daily (Nov–Feb) ⓘ Admission charge

Windsor Castle

Windsor's continued prosperity has a great deal to do with its castle. Known as the oldest and largest occupied castle on the planet, Windsor Castle is one of the Queen's favourite getaways, as evidenced by the frequency with which the monarch's personal standard flies from the Round Tower flagpole. The castle is approximately the same size as 268 tennis courts and feels more like a fortified town than a mere fortress. It's also a significant source of employment and military prowess, and has been a huge draw for sightseers for centuries.

An audio tour – narrated in part by The Prince of Wales – takes you around the castle's attractions in the order they're given below. As you begin, one of the first things pointed out is **The Royal Library**. This has been an integral part of the castle since the reign of King William IV (1830–1837) and is reputed to be the place where William Shakespeare wrote *The Merry Wives of Windsor* at the turn of the 17th century. Shakespeare wrote this in just two weeks after Queen Elizabeth I ordered the writer to create some comic relief, during a time of brutal fighting between Protestants and Catholics in Europe.

Shortly after The Royal Library, visitors reach the breathtaking sight of **Queen Mary's Dolls' House**. Built in 1924, this miniature aristocratic townhouse has running water, electricity and hundreds of accessories. There's even a garden designed by Gertrude Jekyll in a drawer below. In the display units around the house are two remarkable French dolls, presented to the young princesses Elizabeth and Margaret Rose in 1938, along with a number of couture outfits from Cartier and Hermès!

The China Museum is certainly worth a look, if only to admire the extraordinary Rockingham Service commissioned by King William IV in 1830. The intricate designs of the time reflect a sense of pride in the British Empire, with their palm trees, pineapples and coral features. The expense of this undertaking left Yorkshire's Rockingham Works bankrupt.

⬥ *The gorgeous architecture of Windsor Castle*

The **Grand Staircase** and the **Grand Vestibule** are located immediately after the museum. The Grand Staircase, which is adorned with beautifully preserved suits of armour and lit by a glazed gothic lantern roof, leads to the Grand Vestibule and the marble statue of Queen Victoria – depicted here with her favourite collie dog.

The **State Apartments** are a sequence of fine rooms that include the **King's Drawing Room**, the **Queen's Ballroom**, **St George's Hall**, the **Semi-State Apartments** and much more. The visitor exits into **Engine Court**.

Inside **St George's Chapel** all eyes are drawn to the stone, fan-vaulted ceiling, added by King Henry VII (1457–1509). A Perpendicular style dominates, with a huge window and soaring pillars. As you leave, look out for Edward III's 1.8-m (6-ft)-long sword. The daily evensong here at 17.15 is an unforgettable event.

The splendid **Albert Memorial Chapel** is one of the many grand projects commissioned by Queen Victoria as a memorial to her much-loved husband, Albert. It was originally built for Henry III in the 1240s and later altered by George Gilbert Scott at the request of Queen Victoria. Inside, visitors can admire the magnificent marble effigy of Prince Albert by Triqueti.

ⓐ Windsor Castle, High Street ⓣ 020 7766 7304 ⓦ www.royalcollection.org.uk ⓛ 09.45–17.15 daily (Mar–Oct); 09.45–16.15 daily (Nov–Feb) ⓘ Admission charge

RETAIL THERAPY

There are plenty of shopping opportunities to be had in Windsor and the fact that most of them can be enjoyed in car-free, pedestrianised streets is a real bonus. Most of the shops can be split into four key areas – **Windsor Royal Shopping**, **Peascod Street**, **St Leonards Road** and **King Edward Court**. There are also unique boutiques and markets dotted around the town, so anyone who likes a good old-fashioned spree is well catered for.

King Edward Court Running parallel to Peascod Street, and slightly removed from the hustle and bustle, King Edward Court offers a good mix of high-street brands, a large Waitrose supermarket and access to Windsor & Eton Central Rail. There's also a **Fenwick** department store here (ⓐ 10–11 King Edward Court ⓣ 01753 855537 ⓦ www.fenwick.co.uk ⓛ 09.00–18.00 Mon–Sat, 11.00–17.00 Sun).

Markets For stalls selling locally produced organic fare and international treats from farms across Europe, there are only two markets in Windsor worthy of your attention. The first is the **Ascot Farmers' Market**, held in car park three of the racecourse on the third Sunday of each month (ⓛ 09.30–13.00). This is a great place to buy the genetically unmodified produce championed by the Prince of Wales. The **Thames Valley Farmers' Co-operative Market** takes over St Leonards Road on the first Saturday of the month (ⓛ 09.00–13.00). Among the delights on offer, the cake stand is always a spectacular sight to see, smell and taste. Both markets take on a distinctively international feel over the Christmas and Easter holidays.

Peascod Street Ask any Windsor resident where the main shopping strip in Windsor is and they'll point you in the direction of Peascod Street. Here you'll find popular high-street brands including Marks & Spencer, HMV and River Island. There are also a number of stand-alone retail hot spots, equally worthy of your credit card's attention. **Daniel** department store (ⓐ 121–125 Peascod Street ⓣ 01753 801000 ⓦ www.danielstores.co.uk ⓛ 09.30–17.30 Mon & Tues, 09.15–17.30 Wed, 09.30–17.30 Thur–Sat, 11.00–17.00 Sun) has a concession within it to match all moods, and sells everything from thick-knit wool jumpers to celebrity cosmetics.

At **John Goodwin** designer clothes shop (ⓐ 95 Peascod Street ⓣ 01753 866116 ⓦ www.johngoodwin-online.com ⓛ 09.30–18.00 Mon–Sat, 11.00–17.00 Sun), customers can expect made-to-measure orders, home delivery and private evening parties.

🔺 *Treat yourself at the Thames Valley Farmers' Co-operative Market*

St Leonards Road Unusual, unique and irreplaceable is the order of the day at **Rules Antique Interiors** (📍 39 St Leonards Road ☎ 01753 833210 🌐 www.rulesantiques.co.uk 🕐 10.30–18.00 Mon–Sat, closed Sun), where the inventory includes everything from bird cages to weighing scales and antique door knockers to garden statuettes.

If you love cooking and the celebrity chef Anthony Worrall Thompson, then the **Windsor Larder** is a must (📍 59a St Leonards Road ☎ 01753 840272 🌐 www.awt restaurants.com/windsorlarder 🕐 08.00–17.30 Mon–Sat, closed Sun). The principle here is simple. You don't need to be a whizz in the kitchen to eat well, so most of what's sold here is ready to reheat and eat. Expect picnics and dinner parties to take away.

Windsor Royal Shopping This beautiful, historic and sheltered arcade is a great place to start your exploration of Windsor's retail scene. Windsor Royal Shopping is built around the Windsor & Eton Central Rail station and the carefully selected shops within cater for all wants and needs.

For a touch of childhood nostalgia, **Mr Simms Olde Sweet Shoppe** (📍 Royal Station Parade Shopping 🌐 www.mrsimms oldesweetshoppe.co.uk 🕐 09.00–18.00 Mon–Sat, 11.00–17.00 Sun) really hits the spot.

For everything to do with oils, vinegars, spirits, cocktails or liqueurs, head for **VoM Fass** (📍 Royal Station Parade Shopping ☎ 01753 832173 🌐 www.vomfass.com 🕐 10.00–18.00 Mon–Sat, 11.00–17.00 Sun). The stock is stored in oak barrels and mind-boggling bottles.

TAKING A BREAK

CAFÉS

The Crooked House of Windsor £ ❶ Everyone who walks
past this charming tea room does a double take because,
as the name suggests, the building isn't straight. According
to local experts, the extreme lean came about after the wet
timber used to build the house warped as it dried. Aesthetics
aside, this is a lovely, and safe, spot for tea and a toasted
teacake. ➋ 51 High Street ❶ 01753 857534 ❶ 10.00–17.30
Mon–Fri, 10.00–18.30 Sat & Sun

Avanti Bistro Bar Café £–££ ❷ The authentic Italian lasagne is
a stand-out dish at this favourite spot for lunch. ➌ 98 Peascod
Street ❶ 01753 866338 ❶ www.avanti-bistro-cafe.co.uk ❶ 08.30–
18.00 Mon, 08.30–19.00 Tues–Sat, 09.00–18.00 Sun

RESTAURANTS

The Green Olive ££–£££ ❸ Match the size of your dish to your
appetite at this meze-meal restaurant. Dishes include filo
pastries stuffed with spinach and feta, beef casserole in a rich
red-wine sauce and honey and walnut cake. ➋ 10 High Street
❶ 01753 866655 ❶ www.green-olive.co.uk ❶ 12.00–15.00,
18.00–22.30 Mon–Sat, 12.00–15.00, 18.00–22.00 Sun

The Fat Duck £££ ❹ This is the triple-Michelin-starred
brainchild of Heston Blumenthal – a gastronomic hurricane
who adores the science behind cooking. The tasting menu
demands and deserves four hours; the price reflects the quality

⬥ *The accidentally crooked timber-built tea room*

of unforgettable dishes such as salmon poached in liquorice gel and served with an artichoke vanilla mayonnaise. ⓐ High Street, Bray ⓣ 01628 580333 ⓦ www.thefatduck.co.uk ⓛ 12.00–14.00, 19.00–21.30 Tues–Sat, 12.00–14.00 Sun

Strok's Restaurant £££ ❺ This superb restaurant offers amazing views over the river and a refined menu. Expect salads with a sherry dressing, succulent lamb dishes and scrumptious chocolate-box desserts. ⓐ Thames Street ⓣ 01753 861354 ⓦ www.sirchristopherwren.co.uk ⓛ 12.30–14.15, 18.30–21.45 daily

The Waterside Inn £££ ❻ The Roux brothers have been cooking in England since the 1960s and this restaurant – now run by Michel's son Alain – personifies every aspect of the culinary excellence they champion. Dishes range from cocotte of oxtail

🔺 *Confound your tastebuds at The Fat Duck*

and beef cheek braised in Beaujolais wine to date soufflés flavoured with cognac, and served with coffee ice cream. ⓐ Ferry Road, Bray ⓣ 01628 620691 ⓔ reservations@waterside-inn.co.uk ⓛ 12.00–14.00, 19.00–22.00 Wed–Sun (Feb–May & Sept–Dec), 12.00–14.00, 19.00–22.00 Tues–Sun (June–Aug); closed Jan

AFTER DARK

PUBS
The Two Brewers ❼ A homely setting for a quick pint and a cheeky pie. It features ancient oak beams, low ceilings and friendly family dogs. ⓐ 34 Park Street ⓣ 01753 855426 ⓛ 11.30–23.00 Mon–Thur, 11.30–23.30 Fri & Sat, 12.00–22.30 Sun

The Vansittart Arms ❽ Also affectionately known among locals as the Vanny and the Fancy Tart, this friendly pub welcomes all. In the winter patrons are warmed up by roaring, open fires. ⓐ 105 Vansittart Road ⓣ 01753 865988 ⓛ 12.00–23.00 Sun–Wed, 12.00–23.30 Thur, 12.00–24.00 Fri & Sat

THEATRE, MUSIC & COMEDY
The Old Ticket Hall ❾ A top venue for live music and stand-up comedy. ⓐ Windsor & Eton Riverside Rail ⓣ 01753 854554 ⓦ www.oldtickethall.co.uk ⓛ 19.00–02.00 Wed–Sat, 19.00–24.00 Sun, closed Mon & Tues

Theatre Royal ❿ This grand setting dates back to George III (1738–1820). ⓐ Thames Street ⓣ 01753 853888 ⓦ www.theatre royalwindsor.co.uk

Eton

Just over the river from Windsor, the small town of Eton offers visitors an insight into a way of life that hasn't changed all that much over the centuries. The famous Eton College is very much at the core of this community and the High Street is known far and wide for its collection of art galleries, fine dining, superior, tailor-made clothing and intimate bars.

SIGHTS & ATTRACTIONS

The Brocas
These riverbank meadows offer amazing views of Windsor, its castle and life along the River Thames. They're also a great spot for a quiet summer picnic. ⓐ Brocas Street

Coutts & Co
A bank might not seem a likely candidate for a sightseeing to-do list, but Coutts & Co is worthy of a look. Historically, the services of this bank were offered only to the landed gentry and, even though times have changed, prospective clients still need at least £500,000 in disposable funds to open an account. As you might guess from the crowns displayed in the bank's logo, the royal family have an account here. ⓐ Eton High Street

Eton College
Founded by Henry VI in 1440, this school has become one of the best private educational institutes in the world. The college is, of course, a key contributor to the culture of the town, but from

a purely aesthetic point of view a good deal of the school can be enjoyed and photographed without stepping through the front door. From Eton High Street the key sights include the **College Chapel** and the adjoining **Church Yard**, the **Cannon Yard** of the **Geography Department**, the beautiful dome of the **Library** and the **Burning Bush**, a nineteenth-century lamppost on the corner of Eton High Street and Common Lane. This has been a congregation point between lessons for teachers and students for centuries. ⓐ Eton High Street

Eton High Street

If you have 20 minutes to spare and you enjoy a leisurely stroll, a saunter from the beginning of the High Street by the river

◕ Stroll down Eton's picturesque High Street

and up to Eton College is an experience not to be missed. The classic architecture and perfectly preserved wooden shop fronts are a joy to behold and it's easy to lose yourself in the shop windows, which display fine food, antique books and contemporary art. After a few moments wandering along, Eton starts to feel less like a small 21st-century town and more like a quiet, 17th-century village where the pace of life is enjoyably slow.

Millennium sculptures

This series of stainless steel designs by Wendy Ramshaw OBE was commissioned to mark the year 2000. You'll find the stainless-steel bollard sculptures at the beginning of the bridge that connects the town to Windsor. There's also a stand-alone tower bollard with a viewing lens that visitors can aim towards Eton High Street. Take a look through this and see if you can fit in all the sights. Turn around on the same spot and you have a wonderful view of Windsor Castle, rising up over the town and the river below it. ⓐ Windsor Bridge

The Stocks

As you walk along Eton High Street it's not uncommon to see people stopping abruptly to take a second look at something just outside the Tiger Garden Indian restaurant. If you look closely you'll see a set of preserved wooden stocks with metal restraints attached – a device used in the past to incarcerate criminals in a public place. It was hoped that passers-by would think twice about committing a crime if it meant meeting such a humiliating fate! ⓐ 47–49 Eton High Street

Tom Brown Tailors

This traditional tailor's shop was first founded at Number One Eton High Street in 1784. Since then it's been the first port of call for parents looking to equip their children with the correct uniform before they embark on their education at Eton College. The colourful waistcoats designed for the college prefects are an attraction in their own right. ⓐ 1 Eton High Street

The vertical slot postbox

Because of the nearby royal connections, Eton enjoyed many modern conveniences ahead of the rest of the country. This included one of the earliest Victorian postboxes in England – easily identified by the distinct vertical slot. The postbox is still in service to this day, making it the ideal place from which to send a postcard. ⓐ Eton High Street

War Memorial Garden

This garden, halfway along Eton High Street, is dedicated to the memory of the men from Eton who gave their lives for their country in World War I and World War II. The garden is open to all, and more often than not is guarded by a black and white cat, notorious among locals for its daily patrols. ⓐ Eton High Street

CULTURE

Art galleries

Contemporary and classical art are a big part of life in Eton, as anyone who takes a walk along the High Street will soon discover. The price tags attached to some of the offerings on display in the galleries may well leave you breathless, but they are worth a look in all the same. There are plenty of galleries to choose from, but **The Contemporary Fine Art Gallery, The Barker Gallery** and **The Eton Gallery** are popular with residents and visitors alike. ⓐ Eton High Street

Dorney Court

A short journey west of Eton and through the picturesque village of Eton Wick is Dorney Court, a Grade I-listed Tudor manor house. The house has been passed down through 13 generations of the Palmer family over 450 years and is still lived in to this day. Because of this it's only open to the public at certain times of the year, but if your trip to Windsor and Eton

⬥ *Eton is a hub for contemporary art*

happens to coincide, it's well worth the effort. The yearly open days are updated on the Dorney Court website. **ⓐ** Court Lane, Dorney **ⓣ** 01628 604638 **ⓦ** www.dorneycourt.co.uk **ⓔ** palmer@dorneycourt.co.uk **ⓘ** Admission charge

Eton College

Eton College is one of the oldest schools in the United Kingdom and, despite the annual £30,000 attendance fee, places here are fiercely coveted. The school was founded in 1440 by Henry VI to produce the next generation of high-flying scholars, politicians, engineers and explorers, and that's exactly what the college does to this day. Eton has educated 19 British prime ministers, as well as authors George Orwell and Ian Fleming, economist John Maynard Keynes and, more recently, the princes William and Harry – to name but a few. The guided tours of Eton give visitors access to the cobbled school yard, the magnificent **College Chapel**, the classrooms of the lower school and the **Museum of Eton Life**, housed in the former cellar of College Hall.

Certain aspects of the tour are sure to stick in your mind, including the memorials around the Cloisters dedicated to Etonians who gave their lives during wartime, the names of William and Harry etched into the woodwork in the long-standing tradition of graduation from Eton, and the extra-curricular pursuits offered to pupils by their individual tutors: non-examined subjects pursued by students in their spare time include law, medicine, car mechanics and opera! Add to this the cannon in the Geography Department courtyard that was captured in the battle of Sebastopol (1854–5) and the very rare first edition of the Gutenberg Bible (printed in the 1450s) in the college library, and you begin to understand just how special and resourceful Eton College is. ⓐ Eton High Street ☎ 01753 671000 ⓦ www.etoncollege.com ⏱ Tour times vary, see website for details (Mar–Oct) ❶ Admission charge

RETAIL THERAPY

Opportunities for a well-earned spot of retail therapy can be found along the full length of Eton High Street and, as you might expect, you'll find a mix of couture clothing, art galleries (serving champagne to their clients) and delicious delicatessens.

C J Reid This chemist and wine merchant is a kitsch treat for any shopper and a practical stop for over-the-counter medicines and remedies. ⓐ 30 Eton High Street ☎ 01753 863819 ⏱ 09.00–18.00 Mon–Sat, closed Sun

Eton Antique Bookshop If rare and second-hand books are your thing, then the stacks of wonderfully aromatic treasures in this shop are guaranteed to excite. ⓐ 88 Eton High Street ☎ 01753 855534 ⏱ 11.30–18.00 Mon–Fri, 11.00–19.00 Sat, 12.00–18.00 Sun (hours may vary)

Jack Wills The clothes on sale here are a mix of high-street chic and wonderfully posh casual attire. Expect thick-knit cashmere jumpers, polo shirts galore and effervescent underwear. ⓐ 17 Eton High Street ☎ 01753 856112 ⓦ www.jackwills.com ⏱ 10.00–18.00 Mon–Sat, 11.00–17.00 Sun

TAKING A BREAK

Zero.3 £ ⓫ The menu at this coffee and sandwich bar offers a good selection of hearty fare and is great value for money. ⓐ 45 Eton High Street ⓣ 01753 864725 ⓛ 07.30–16.00 Mon–Fri, 08.30–17.00 Sat, 10.30–16.00 Sun

Tastes Delicatessen £–££ ⓬ This deli sells a mind-boggling variety of cooked meats, cheese, stuffed olives, tangy pickles and cake. There's also a good selection of gluten-, dairy- and nut-free dishes. ⓐ 92 Eton High Street ⓣ 01753 641557 ⓦ www.tastesdeli.co.uk ⓛ 10.30–18.00 Tues, 10.30–19.00 Wed, 10.30–18.00 Thur & Fri, 10.00–18.00 Sat, closed Sun & Mon

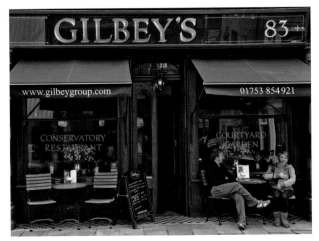

▲ *A fashionable favourite for fine dining*

Gilbey's ££–£££ ⓲ *Vogue* magazine loves Gilbey's for a reason and that might be something to do with the fillet of Cornish hake roasted with coriander seed butter, the lemon pilaf and the fennel compôte, among other menu selections! ⓐ 82–83 Eton High Street ⓣ 01753 854921 ⓦ www.gilbeygroup.com ⓔ eton@gilbeygroup.com ⓛ 12.00–14.30, 18.00–21.30 Sun–Fri, 12.00–14.30, 18.00–22.00 Sat

AFTER DARK

The George Inn ⓴ If you're in town in the summer, then head for the terrace at The George Inn. This historic, 300-year-old pub is a great place for a glass of wine, a pint or, if you're feeling decadent, a chilled bottle of bubbly. ⓐ 77 Eton High Street ⓣ 01753 861797 ⓛ 10.00–23.30 Sun–Fri, 10.00–24.00 Sat

The Henry VI ⓯ With live music most weekends, a spacious beer garden and traditional British grub on the menu, The Henry VI is a popular everyday spot. ⓐ 37 Eton High Street ⓣ 01753 866051 ⓛ 12.00–23.30 Sun–Thur, 12.00–24.00 Fri & Sat

The Watermans Arms ⓰ Originally a workhouse back in 1542, this building became a makeshift mortuary during the Great Plague. Today it's a traditional English pub with a popular comedy club attached. ⓐ Brocas Street ⓣ 01753 861001 ⓦ www.watermans-eton.com ⓛ 18.00–24.00 Mon, 12.00–23.00 Tues–Fri, 12.00–24.00 Sat, 12.00–23.30 Sun

---

▶ *Cliveden Estate's beautifully manicured lawn*

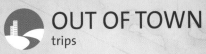

OUT OF TOWN
trips

Maidenhead

Maidenhead is the largest town in the Royal Borough and, thanks to the well-developed transport links, it's easy to nip to for shopping, celebrity-spotting and gallery exhibitions.

GETTING THERE

By bus
Local buses are cost-effective and efficient. Bus No 6 goes to Maidenhead via Bray and takes just under an hour.

By car
Take the A308 from Windsor straight to Maidenhead. The drive should take less than 20 minutes.

Tourist information
The Maidenhead Information Centre has up-to-date listings for all of the cultural comings and goings in town. You'll find the centre in the Central Library. ⓐ St Ives Road ❶ 01628 796502 ⓔ maidenhead.tic@rbwm.gov.uk ⓛ 09.30–17.00 Mon, 09.30–20.00 Tues, 09.30–17.00 Wed, 09.30–20.00 Thur, 09.30–19.00 Fri, 09.30–16.00 Sat, closed Sun

SIGHTS & ATTRACTIONS

Boutler's Lock
This lock, dating back to 1772, is a popular spot for kayakers and canoeists. Regular buses connect this scenic area to

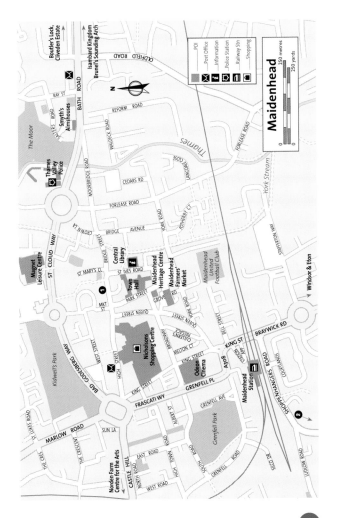

Maidenhead

POI
Post Office
Information
Police Station
Railway Stn
Shopping

250 metres
250 yards

Maidenhead town centre and, even if watersports aren't your thing, there are plenty of parkland attractions to be enjoyed nearby on Ray Mill Island. ⓐ Lower Cookham Road

Cliveden Estate

Close to Ray Mill Island, the estate is immediately recognisable by the beech woods on the steep cliffs, 200 m (650 ft) above the river. The house at Cliveden was made famous when Lady Astor lived there and today the 152-ha (376-acre) estate is protected and preserved by the National Trust. Highlights include a beautiful water garden and the spectacular views along the woodland walk. ⓐ Taplow ⓣ 01494 755562 ⓦ www.nationaltrust.org.uk/cliveden ⓘ Admission charge

Isambard Kingdom Brunel's Sounding Arch

This stunning brick railway bridge, designed by the famous civil engineer, was finished in 1838; it still carries trains over the River Thames. Over the towpath on the left, just downstream of Maidenhead Bridge, is the Sounding Arch – test how many times your voice echoes as you shout out beneath it. The bridge is commemorated in *Rain, Steam and Speed*, an 1844 painting by J M W Turner. ⓐ Downriver of Boulter's Lock, near Bath Road

Maidenhead river walks

A stroll along the riverbanks from Maidenhead will take keen hikers to the nearby villages of Cookham and Marlow (upstream) and Bray, Eton and Windsor (downstream). A walk through nearby Maidenhead Thicket is also worthwhile; it is known to have been the old haunt of highwayman Dick Turpin.

CULTURE

Maidenhead Heritage Centre

The Maidenhead Heritage Centre traces the story of the settlement back to the Romans. There are photo albums galore of days gone by, free lunchtime lectures twice a month and a number of exhibitions. This is also a great place to pick up local maps and books. ⓐ 18 Park Street ⓣ 01628 780555 ⓦ www.maidenheadheritage.org.uk ⓛ 10.00–16.00 Tues–Sat, 10.00–12.30 every second Sun of the month, closed Mon

Norden Farm Centre for the Arts

Ten years old in 2010, the Norden Farm Centre for the Arts is Maidenhead's cultural pride and joy. The venue offers a programme brimming with cutting-edge entertainment and performing arts. From touring productions and endorsements from Sir Michael Parkinson to literature festivals and dance societies, you'll find it here. Performances take place in the large Courtyard Theatre, the 100-person capacity Studio Theatre and the intimate Long Barn. There's also a free art gallery to the rear. ⓐ Altwood Road ⓣ 01628 682555 ⓦ www.nordenfarm.org ⓘ Admission charge

Odeon Cinema

This eight-screen movie theatre showcases all the latest Hollywood blockbusters, which you can enjoy from the comfort of the special, body-sculpted seats. ⓐ 42–44 King Street ⓣ 0871 224 4007 ⓦ www.odeon.co.uk ⓘ Admission charge

◓ *Delightful sculptures in the grounds of Cliveden Estate*

RETAIL THERAPY

Maidenhead Farmers' Market This popular spot sells the best local produce, every second Sunday of the month. You'll find the 25 stalls in the Grove Road car park behind Maidenhead Town Hall between 10.00 and 13.00 – selling fresh fish, local meats, bakery treats, vegetables and cider. ⓐ Grove Road

Nicholsons Shopping Centre All of the big high-street brands can be found in this shopping centre. ⓐ Nicholsons Walk ⓣ 01628 783746 ⓦ www.nicholsonsshoppingcentre.co.uk ⓛ 09.00–17.30 Mon–Sat, 11.00–17.00 Sun

TAKING A BREAK

Hobgoblin £–££ ❶ This is a friendly and modern ale house with a pleasant garden and a lively atmosphere. It's also a popular spot on the local ghost-tour circuit, so keep an eye out for ghouls, especially when closing time approaches. ⓐ 34 High Street ⓣ 01628 784786 ⓛ 11.30–23.00 Mon–Sat, 11.00–23.00 Sun

Fredrick's Hotel ££–£££ ❷ The hotel restaurant Alfresco is a real treat, but it won't break the bank and the setting is perfect for any special occasion. From the classic house club sandwich to the prawn and chilli salsa and coconut rice parcels, there's a dish here to put a smile on your face. ⓐ Shoppenhangers Road ⓣ 01628 581000 ⓦ www.fredricks-hotel.co.uk ⓛ 07.00–09.30, 12.00–14.00, 19.00–21.30 Sun–Fri, 07.00–09.30, 19.00–21.30 Sat

Richmond upon Thames

If you like the scenery and the pace of life in Windsor, then you'll like this borough of London. Richmond upon Thames boasts a number of very special attractions, including Hampton Court Palace, Kew Gardens, the culture-rich Richmond Park and some stunning views of London.

GETTING THERE

By car

From Windsor take the M4 east until you reach the roundabout before junction 1. Follow Chiswick High Road, which becomes Kew Road, and go over the River Thames. Kew Road then becomes Twickenham Road, at which point you've reached Richmond upon Thames.

By train

From Windsor & Eton Riverside it is possible to travel direct to Richmond on the train destined ultimately for London Waterloo. The journey from Windsor to Richmond takes 36 minutes. From Richmond, London is only 15 minutes away by train.

Tourist information

You can find up-to-date information about everything in the borough at the **Richmond Visitor Information Centre**, located in the Old Town Hall. ❸ Whittaker Avenue, just off George Street ❶ 0208 734 3363 ❿ www.visitrichmond.co.uk ❷ info@visit richmond.co.uk ❸ 10.00–17.00 Mon–Sat, closed Sun

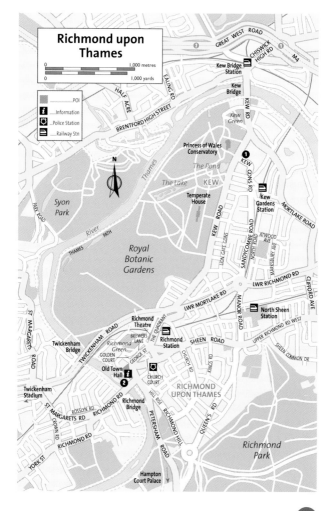

SIGHTS & ATTRACTIONS

Hampton Court Palace

This extraordinary building, lavishly rebuilt by Cardinal Wolsey in the early 16th century and acquired by King Henry VIII, is within easy striking distance of Richmond and is a must-see attraction. The 24 ha (60 acres) of beautiful riverside gardens, the world-famous maze and the sumptuous interiors are a magnificent snapshot in time of Henry's ostentatious character. Hampton Court Palace is a short journey south from Richmond. ⓐ Hampton Court Road ⓦ www.hrp.org.uk/hamptoncourt palace ⓔ hamptoncourt@hrp.org.uk ⓛ 10.00–18.00 daily (Apr–Sept); 10.00–16.30 daily (Oct–Mar) ⓘ Admission charge

Richmond Park

At 1,012 ha (2,500 acres), this is the largest royal park in London and home to 600 free-roaming deer. There's a golf course, and from King Henry's Mound there are spectacular views of St Paul's Cathedral and the London skyline, 16 km (10 miles) away. ⓐ Richmond Park ⓣ 020 8948 3209 ⓦ www.royalparks.org.uk ⓛ Dawn to dusk daily

Royal Botanic Gardens, Kew

You can't pass through Richmond without taking a trip to Kew Gardens – it has one of the most impressive collections of plant life in the world and is a certified World Heritage Site. In addition to the *ginormous* water lilies and the stunning greenhouse collections, the site is also an important botanical research centre, championing conservation around the world. ⓐ Kew Road

📞 020 8332 5655 🌐 www.kew.org ⏱ Opening times vary: see website for details ❗ Admission charge

CULTURE

Richmond Theatre

The interior of this beautiful red-brick and stone building is a mix of box seats, felt-covered chairs and carved cherubs. From Billie Piper in breakthrough roles to the hilarious Christmas pantomimes, the annual programme has something for everyone. The theatre is also popular with filmmakers and was featured in the films *Finding Neverland* and *Evita*. ⓐ The Green 📞 0870 060 6651 🌐 www.ambassador tickets.com/Richmond-Theatre ❗ Admission charge

🔻 *Views across the enticing woodland of Richmond Park*

Twickenham Stadium

A real treat for any rugby union fan, this stadium can hold 82,000 spectators and is the undisputed home of English rugby union. It's also the biggest rugby union stadium on the planet and over the years has become a popular music venue, attracting big names and big crowds. Visitors here can also enjoy the **Museum of Rugby** and take part in stadium tours. ⓐ Rugby Road ⓣ 0871 222 2120 ⓦ www.rfu.com/TwickenhamStadium

RETAIL THERAPY

Visitors to Richmond are spoilt for choice with shops, boutiques, one-of-a-kind retailers and commercial art galleries galore. The highest concentration of such shops can be found in **Church Court**, **Hill Rise**, **Brewers Lane** and **Golden Court**.

TAKING A BREAK

The Original Maids of Honour £–££ ❶ You'll find this little tea room opposite Kew Gardens serving up an irresistible selection of cakes, cookies, tea and coffee. ⓐ 288 Kew Road, Kew ⓣ 020 8940 2752 ⓒ 09.00–18.00 Mon–Sat, 08.30–18.00 Sun

Tide Tables £–££ ❷ A scenic spot for vegetarian light bites or more substantial dishes under the arches of Richmond Bridge. The large outdoor terrace is lovely in summer. ⓐ Arch 2, Richmond Riverside ⓣ 020 8948 8285 ⓒ 08.30–18.30 daily

ⓞ *Even Windsor's information centre is delightfully housed*

PRACTICAL
information

Directory

GETTING THERE

By air

Because of Windsor's proximity to London, flying into town from destinations around the world – and indeed from within the UK – is simple. With the train links into the British capital, Luton, Stansted and Gatwick Airport are all within easy striking distance; however Heathrow Airport is the closest to Windsor. Heathrow is served by every major airline and many smaller operators. It is directly linked to Windsor by local bus services and by the National Express coach network.

British Airways ☎ 0844 493 0787 Ⓦ www.britishairways.com
EasyJet ☎ 0871 244 2366 Ⓦ www.easyjet.com
Thomas Cook ☎ 0871 230 2406
Ⓦ http://book.flythomascook.com
Virgin Atlantic ☎ 0844 874 7747 Ⓦ www.virgin-atlantic.com

Many people are aware that air travel emits CO_2, which contributes to climate change. You may be interested in lessening the environmental impact of your flight through the charity **Climate Care** (Ⓦ www.jpmorganclimatecare.com), which offsets your CO_2 by funding environmental projects around the world.

By car

When you arrive in Windsor you'll soon discover that you don't really need a car to get around; however, the town is well connected to Britain's national road infrastructure. Windsor is linked to the M4 via junction 6, the M3 via junction 3, the M25 via junction 13 and the M40 via junction 4 or junction 2.

By train

Windsor is connected to the British railway network, with two stations linking the town to wherever you might need to go. With a quick change at Slough, London can be reached in less than 40 minutes, making Windsor a very attractive day-trip destination for visitors arriving into London's airports and the Eurostar terminus at King's Cross St Pancras. All timetables and information about which destinations are linked to Windsor by rail can be accessed through Network Rail. ☎ 0845 748 4950 ⓦ www.networkrail.co.uk

By bus and coach

For travel information about local bus services operating in Windsor, Eton and the surrounding area, and to plan your journey in advance, go to the **First Group** website. ⓦ www.firstgroup.com

You can find out more about the Green Line coach service between London and Windsor by calling their help centre or looking online. The timetables, fares and booking facilities for National Express coach services operating in the area are also available online.

Green Line coach services ☎ 0844 801 7261 ⓦ www.greenline.co.uk

National Express coach services ⓦ www.nationalexpress.com

HEALTH, SAFETY & CRIME

The NHS community hospital in Windsor is **King Edward VII Hospital** on St Leonards Road (☎ 01753 860441). If you require a General Practitioner try the **Dedworth Medical Centre** (◉ 300 Dedworth Road ☎ 01753 864545).

If you need police assistance you can find the station on **Alma Road** (☎ 08458 505505).

If you require a dentist during your trip to Windsor, try the **Oakleigh Dental Surgery** (◉ 34a Alma Road ☎ 01753 861161).

OPENING HOURS

The shops in Windsor are generally open between 09.30 and 18.00 from Monday to Saturday, with slightly shorter opening hours on a Sunday. It's not uncommon to find that smaller businesses are only open for one day over the weekend.

The primary tourist attractions in the town are usually open 10.00–17.00, closing slightly earlier on Sundays.

Banks in Windsor are normally open 09.00–17.00 Monday to Friday and 09.00–noon on Saturdays, closed on Sundays.

TOILETS

You can find toilets open to the public in the King Edward Court shopping area. Alternatively, head to the toilets inside the Fenwick department store, next to the hair salon.

CHILDREN

Many of the attractions in Windsor are suited to children, especially plastic-fantastic **Legoland** (see page 56). The following is also particularly good:

Windsor Leisure Centre A great riverside spot with a wave machine, a children's crèche and an adventure play-zone. ⓐ Stovell Road ☎ 01753 778566 🕐 10.00–21.30 Mon & Tues, 10.00–22.00 Wed, 10.00–21.30 Thur & Fri, 10.00–18.00 Sat, 10.00–16.00 Sun. Please note that from 18.15 to 22.00 the centre is open to over-21s only.

TRAVELLERS WITH DISABILITIES

Because of the historic nature of the Royal Borough, there are a number of inherent problems for travellers with disabilities. Many attractions, including Windsor Castle, the Theatre Royal and Eton College, offer specialist access and assistance, but others are on steep hills and are less accessible to wheelchair users because of the old architecture. A full access guide is available on request from the **Royal Windsor Information Centre** (☎ 01753 743900). You can also find information online: ⓦ www.windsor.gov.uk/site/visitor-info/travelling-with-a-disability

Wheelchair-friendly taxis operate from the primary taxi rank on Windsor High Street. You can also call the taxi rank directly (☎ 01753 862020) to pre-book a wheelchair-accessible vehicle.

FURTHER INFORMATION

For information head to the Old Ticket Hall in Windsor & Eton Central Rail, part of the Windsor Royal Shopping arcade. **Royal Windsor Information Centre** ☎ 01753 743900 ⓦ www.windsor.gov.uk ⓔ windsor.tic@rbwm.gov.uk 🕐 09.30–17.30 Mon–Sat, 10.00–16.00 Sun (Mar–Oct); 10.00–17.00 Mon–Sat, 10.00–16.00 Sun (Nov–Feb)

ACKNOWLEDGEMENTS
The photographs in this book were taken.by Grant Rooney for Thomas Cook Publishing, to whom the copyright belongs.

Project editor: Kate Taylor
Layout: Donna Pedley
Proofreaders: Ting Baker & Emily Anderson
Indexer: Mary Purton

AUTHOR BIOGRAPHY
Robert Savage is a member of the British Guild of Travel Writers. In addition to writing guidebooks he also contributes to *The Guardian*, MSN and several in-flight magazines. In Windsor Robert enjoys nothing more than a pot of coffee in The Crooked House of Windsor and a long stroll through Windsor Great Park.

Send your thoughts to
books@thomascook.com

- Found a great bar, club, shop or must-see sight that we don't feature?
- Like to tip us off about any information that needs a little updating?
- Want to tell us what you love about this handy little guidebook and more importantly how we can make it even handier?

Then here's your chance to tell all! Send us ideas, discoveries and recommendations today and then look out for your valuable input in the next edition of this title.

Email the above address (stating the title) or write to:
pocket guides Series Editor, Thomas Cook Publishing, PO Box 227, Coningsby Road, Peterborough PE3 8SB, UK.